Cooking Light®

Our Best
Low Carb
Recipes

Published by Oxmoor House, Inc.
ISBN: 0-8487-2931-5
Printed in the United States of America

Contents

Be sure to check with your health-care provider before making any changes in your diet.

Front Cover: Baked Flounder with Fresh Lemon Pepper *(page 16)*

Back Cover: Rosemary-Grilled Veal Chops *(page 27)*, Southern-Style Shrimp *(page 22)*, and Spiced Pepper-Crusted Filet Mignon with Asparagus *(page 25)*

Introduction

The research is inconclusive as to the long-term health benefits of low-carbohydrate diets. However, people are quickly and successfully losing weight following a variety of low- and modified-carb eating plans. And, in the short-term, there appear to be no harmful side effects.

Although *Cooking Light* does not necessarily embrace the low-carb philosophy as a lifetime weight control solution, the editors realize that some readers may choose to follow a low-carb diet. The magazine can help, since every recipe in *Cooking Light* has a complete nutrient analysis that includes the grams of total carbohydrate and fiber. Readers have the option of choosing recipes that are low in carbohydrate with the guarantee that the recipes have passed the rigorous *Cooking Light* Test Kitchens flavor test.

So, for the first time, *Cooking Light* has gathered some of its best low-carbohydrate recipes in one easy-to-use cookbook. Whether you're already counting carbs or just starting a low-carb plan, *Cooking Light Our Best Low Carb Recipes* is for you. The book features over 50 great-tasting, easy-to-prepare recipes for breakfast, lunch, dinner, and snacks. Most recipes have less than 5 grams of carbohydrate per serving, although some (those recipes that include veggies) range between 5 to 10 grams of carbohydrate per serving.

In keeping with the *Cooking Light* philosophy of healthy eating, recipes use lower fat cuts of pork and beef, fish, and poultry. Many emphasize the heart-healthy fats, such as the monounsaturated fat in olive oil and the omega-3 fat in salmon. Several recipes call for vitamin-rich vegetables such as spinach, kale, green beans, asparagus, and salad greens—all options on even the lowest carb diets. The philosophy that *Cooking Light* will continue to embrace is eating smart and living well—and these recipes will help you do just that.

Breakfast Scramble

Carb 3.7g

Calories 94
(36% from fat)
Fat 3.6g
(sat 1.5g)
Protein 10.9g
Fiber 0.5g
Chol 110mg
Iron 1.7mg
Sodium 205mg
Calcium 83mg

If you choose to use real eggs, count on 1 large egg for each ¼ cup of egg substitute.

Cooking spray
¾ cup chopped seeded tomato
¼ cup chopped green bell pepper
¼ cup sliced green onions
3 large eggs
1½ cups egg substitute
¼ cup fat-free milk
¼ cup (1 ounce) shredded reduced-fat Cheddar cheese
⅛ teaspoon black pepper
⅛ teaspoon hot sauce

1. Heat a large nonstick skillet coated with cooking spray over medium-high heat. Add tomato, green bell pepper, and green onions; sauté until tender. Remove mixture from skillet and set aside.

2. Combine eggs and next 5 ingredients in a large bowl; beat well with a wire whisk. Pour mixture into skillet, and cook over low heat, stirring gently. Cook until mixture is firm, but still moist. Remove from heat. Stir in vegetable mixture. Serve immediately. **Yield:** 6 servings.

Spinach Frittata

Some marinara sauces are much lower in carbohydrate than others—check the nutrient labels to compare. We found that Contadina Deluxe Marinara Sauce has one of the lower carb counts.

2	teaspoons butter
½	cup chopped onion
1	garlic clove, minced
1½	cups egg substitute
¼	teaspoon salt
¼	teaspoon black pepper
⅛	teaspoon ground nutmeg
1	(10-ounce) package frozen chopped spinach, thawed, drained, and squeezed dry
½	cup (2 ounces) shredded Swiss cheese
1	cup warm fat-free marinara sauce

Carb 6.9g

Calories 154
(30% from fat)
Fat 5.1g
(sat 2.3g)
Protein 15.9g
Fiber 3.7g
Chol 10mg
Iron 3.5mg
Sodium 580mg
Calcium 223mg

1. Melt butter in a 10-inch nonstick skillet with sloped sides over medium-high heat. Add onion and garlic; sauté until tender.

2. Combine egg substitute and next 4 ingredients; add onion mixture, stirring well. Pour egg mixture into skillet. Cover; cook over medium-low heat 10 minutes or until mixture is set. Remove from heat; sprinkle with cheese. Cover; let stand 5 minutes or until cheese melts. Serve with warm marinara sauce. **Yield:** 4 servings.

Cheesy Zucchini Frittata

If you like omelets, you'll love frittatas. They're easier to make because all the ingredients are stirred into the eggs and cooked together.

½   cup (2 ounces) shredded part-skim mozzarella cheese
½   cup finely chopped green onions
¼   cup (1 ounce) grated fresh Parmesan cheese
¼   cup chopped fresh basil
¼   teaspoon black pepper
⅛   teaspoon salt
6   large egg whites
2   large eggs
1   teaspoon olive oil
1½ cups thinly sliced zucchini
½   cup chopped green bell pepper

1. Preheat oven to 475°.

2. Combine first 8 ingredients in a bowl; stir well with a whisk.

3. Heat oil in a nonstick skillet over medium-high heat. Add zucchini and bell pepper; sauté 5 minutes. Add egg mixture. Reduce heat to low; cook 5 minutes or until set around edges. Remove pan from heat.

4. Wrap handle of pan with foil. Bake at 475° for 8 minutes or until center is set. **Yield:** 4 servings (serving size: 1 wedge).

Asparagus and Basil Omelet

Use fat-free, cholesterol-free egg substitute to add volume to the omelet. This ingredient is a great time-saver because it takes the place of separating egg whites. (Egg substitute provides about 2 grams carbohydrate per ½ cup, while real eggs are carbohydrate-free.)

Cooking spray
12 asparagus spears, diagonally cut into 1-inch pieces (about 1 cup)
 2 large eggs
 ½ cup egg substitute
 ¼ cup water
 ½ teaspoon salt
 ¼ teaspoon coarsely ground black pepper
 2 tablespoons chopped fresh basil
 ¼ cup (1 ounce) shredded Swiss cheese

Carb 5.4g

Calories 172
(47% from fat)
Fat 8.9g
(sat 4g)
Protein 17.7g
Fiber 1.6g
Chol 225mg
Iron 2.6mg
Sodium 812mg
Calcium 195mg

1. Heat a nonstick skillet coated with cooking spray over medium-high heat. Add asparagus, and sauté 3 minutes; set aside.

2. Combine eggs and next 4 ingredients in a medium bowl; whisk until blended.

3. Wipe pan with paper towels; recoat with cooking spray, and heat over medium heat. Add egg mixture, and cook 3 minutes or until set (do not stir). Sprinkle with asparagus, basil, and cheese. Loosen omelet with spatula; fold in half. Cook 1 to 2 minutes or until egg mixture is set and cheese melts. Slide omelet onto a plate; cut in half. **Yield:** 2 servings (serving size: ½ omelet).

Confetti Cheese Omelet

Carb 6.5g

Calories 165
(34% from fat)
Fat 6.1g
(sat 4g)
Protein 20g
Fiber 1.1g
Chol 20mg
Iron 2.3mg
Sodium 786mg
Calcium 254mg

Great for breakfast but hearty enough for dinner, omelets are an easy option any night of the week.

Cooking spray
¼ cup chopped red bell pepper
¼ cup chopped green or orange bell pepper
¼ cup sliced green onions
1 cup egg substitute
¼ teaspoon salt
¼ teaspoon freshly ground black pepper
½ cup (2 ounces) shredded reduced-fat Cheddar cheese

1. Heat a 10-inch nonstick skillet coated with cooking spray over medium heat. Add peppers and green onions; cook 4 minutes, stirring occasionally.

2. Pour egg substitute into skillet; sprinkle with salt and pepper. Cook, without stirring, 2 to 3 minutes or until golden brown on bottom. Sprinkle with cheese. Loosen omelet with a spatula; fold in half. Cook 2 additional minutes or until egg mixture is set and cheese begins to melt. Slide omelet onto a plate; cut in half. **Yield:** 2 servings (serving size: ½ omelet).

※**Creative Omelets:** Use your imagination to create your own variations. Sautéed vegetables, salsas, and tomato mixtures flavored with herbs all make delectable, low-carb fillings for omelets. Spread about ⅓ to ½ cup filling over half of the cooked omelet, and fold over.

Crustless Spinach Quiche

Omitting the pastry crust from a quiche saves approximately 11 grams of carbohydrate per serving.

Carb 5.4g

Calories 198
(47% from fat)
Fat 10.4g
(sat 6.7g)
Protein 19.6g
Fiber 1.5g
Chol 29mg
Iron 1.2mg
Sodium 412mg
Calcium 486mg

3 ounces ⅓-less-fat cream cheese, softened
1 cup fat-free milk
1 cup egg substitute
¼ teaspoon black pepper
3 cups (12 ounces) shredded reduced-fat
   Cheddar cheese
Cooking spray
1 (10-ounce) package frozen chopped spinach,
   thawed, drained, and squeezed dry
1 (10-ounce) package frozen chopped broccoli,
   thawed, drained, and squeezed dry
1 small onion, finely chopped
5 fresh whole mushrooms, sliced
Salsa (optional)

1. Preheat oven to 350°.

2. Beat cream cheese in a large bowl with a mixer at medium speed until creamy. Add milk, egg substitute, and pepper; beat until smooth. Stir in cheese.

3. Heat a large nonstick skillet coated with cooking spray over medium heat. Cook spinach and next 3 ingredients just until tender and liquid evaporates. Cool slightly.

4. Combine milk mixture and spinach mixture, stirring well. Pour into a 10-inch quiche dish coated with cooking spray. Bake, uncovered, at 350° for 45 to 50 minutes or until center is set. Remove from oven, and cool on a wire rack 10 minutes.

5. Serve quiche with salsa, if desired (salsa not included in analysis). **Yield:** 8 servings (serving size: 1 wedge).

Crispy Salmon with Herb Salad

Carb 1.4g

Calories 303
(49% from fat)
Fat 16.4g
(sat 2.8g)
Protein 35.4g
Fiber 0.6g
Chol 111mg
Iron 1.4mg
Sodium 286mg
Calcium 35mg

Place salmon fillets atop fresh herbs tossed with a light lemon dressing. For best results, use small basil and mint leaves; if you have only large leaves, tear them in half. Refrigerate the herb mixture before preparing the salmon so it won't wilt.

1½ cups arugula leaves
¾ cup fresh flat-leaf parsley leaves
½ cup fresh cilantro leaves
½ cup small fresh basil leaves
¼ cup small fresh mint leaves
1 tablespoon fresh lemon juice
1 tablespoon extravirgin olive oil
½ teaspoon salt, divided
½ teaspoon freshly ground black pepper, divided
1 garlic clove, minced
Cooking spray
6 (6-ounce) salmon fillets, skinned
6 lemon wedges

1. Combine first 5 ingredients in a large bowl. Cover and refrigerate.

2. Combine juice, oil, ¼ teaspoon salt, ¼ teaspoon pepper, and garlic, stirring with a whisk.

3. Heat a large nonstick skillet coated with cooking spray over medium heat. Sprinkle salmon with ¼ teaspoon salt and ¼ teaspoon pepper. Add fillets to pan; cook 9 minutes or until fish flakes easily when tested with a fork, turning once. Combine arugula mixture and juice mixture; toss well to coat. Place ½ cup herb salad on each of 6 plates; top each serving with 1 fillet. Serve with lemon wedges. **Yield:** 6 servings.

Seared Tuna with Arugula Salad

4	(6-ounce) yellowfin tuna steaks (about ¾ inch thick)
1½	teaspoons freshly ground black pepper, divided
¾	teaspoon kosher salt, divided
2	tablespoons olive oil, divided
2	tablespoons fresh lemon juice
8	cups arugula leaves
2	cups thinly sliced fennel bulb (about 1 small bulb)

Carb 6.9g
Calories 276
(29% from fat)
Fat 8.8g
(sat 1.3g)
Protein 41.7g
Fiber 2g
Chol 77mg
Iron 2.3mg
Sodium 544mg
Calcium 124mg

1. Sprinkle tuna steaks with 1 teaspoon pepper and ¼ teaspoon salt. Heat 1 tablespoon oil in a large nonstick skillet over medium-high heat. Add tuna steaks; cook 2 minutes on each side or until desired degree of doneness.

2. Combine ½ teaspoon pepper, ½ teaspoon salt, 1 tablespoon oil, and juice in a large bowl; stir with a whisk. Add arugula and fennel; toss well. Place about 2 cups salad on each of 4 plates; top each serving with 1 tuna steak. **Yield:** 4 servings.

※**The Virtues of Olive Oil:** All olive oils are rich in monounsaturated fat, a healthier choice than saturated types. Plus, olive oils outdistance vegetable oils in flavor. For the most flavor, use high-quality extravirgin olive oil instead of virgin or light olive oil, especially in salad dressings and for sautéing.

Seafood Salad

Carb 6.7g

Calories 158
(13% from fat)
Fat 2.2g
(sat 0.4g)
Protein 27g
Fiber 1.6g
Chol 136mg
Iron 2.9mg
Sodium 261mg
Calcium 107mg

1	pound medium shrimp, peeled and deveined
½	pound sea scallops
½	pound lump crabmeat, shell pieces removed
1½	cups chopped seeded tomato (about 1 pound)
¼	cup minced fresh cilantro
3	tablespoons minced shallots or green onions
3	tablespoons fresh lime juice
1	tablespoon minced seeded jalapeño pepper
6	cups gourmet salad greens

1. Steam shrimp and scallops, covered, 6 minutes or until done; cool.

2. Cut shrimp and scallops into quarters. Combine shrimp, scallops, crabmeat, and next 5 ingredients in a bowl. Serve over salad greens. **Yield:** 6 servings (serving size: 1 cup seafood mixture and 1 cup salad greens).

＊**Sassy Cilantro:** Cilantro is a cosmopolitan herb. The pungent parsley lookalike is routinely sprinkled into soups in Cambodia, dabbled over curries in India, mixed into salsas in Mexico, and stirred into salads in Israel. This widespread favorite gained popularity in American kitchens relatively recently as a key element of Mexican fare. Cooks quickly embraced its distinctive grassy flavor.

The benefits of cilantro go beyond taste: A tablespoon of cilantro jazzes up any dish, adding less than a calorie and offering a good bit of the daily value of vitamin A. Since it's susceptible to heat, cilantro is at its best in cold dishes or added just before serving.

Spicy Beef Salad

1	(1-pound) flank steak, trimmed
	Cooking spray
⅓	cup sliced shallots
¼	cup chopped fresh cilantro
3	tablespoons fresh lime juice
1	tablespoon fish sauce
2	teaspoons sliced Thai red chiles or serrano chiles
2	medium tomatoes, cut into ¼-inch-thick wedges (about ¾ pound)

Carb 7.6g

Calories 214
(39% from fat)
Fat 9.2g
(sat 3.9g)
Protein 25g
Fiber 1.1g
Chol 59mg
Iron 2.8mg
Sodium 407mg
Calcium 17mg

1. Prepare grill or broiler.

2. Place steak on a grill rack or broiler pan coated with cooking spray; grill 6 minutes on each side or until desired degree of doneness.

3. Cut steak diagonally across the grain into thin slices; cut each slice into 2-inch pieces.

4. Combine steak, shallots, and remaining ingredients, and toss gently. **Yield:** 4 servings (serving size: 1 cup).

Grilled Chicken Greek Salad

Carb 6.2g

Calories 236
(51% from fat)
Fat 13.5g
(sat 3.4g)
Protein 23.8g
Fiber 2.2g
Chol 61mg
Iron 2mg
Sodium 1215mg
Calcium 76mg

Regular, "full-fat" salad dressings are usually lower in carbohydrate than reduced-fat and fat-free versions.

1 (10-ounce) package torn romaine lettuce (about 8 cups)
2 (6-ounce) packages grilled chicken breast strips (such as Louis Rich)
2 large plum tomatoes, chopped
½ cup sliced cucumber
¼ cup chopped pitted kalamata olives or chopped ripe olives
½ cup (2 ounces) reduced-fat crumbled feta cheese
⅓ cup Greek dressing (such as Ken's with feta, black olives, and olive oil)
Freshly ground black pepper

1. Combine all ingredients in a large bowl; toss gently to coat. Serve immediately. **Yield:** 4 servings (serving size: 3 cups).

Curried Chicken Salad

Carb 3.1g

Calories 134
(44% from fat)
Fat 6.5g
(sat 1.4g)
Protein 15.6g
Fiber 0.4g
Chol 49mg
Iron 0.8mg
Sodium 730mg
Calcium 8mg

2 (6-ounce) packages grilled chicken strips, chopped
½ cup chopped celery
¼ cup low-fat mayonnaise
2 tablespoons fresh lemon juice
1 teaspoon curry powder
⅛ teaspoon coarsely ground black pepper

1. Combine all ingredients in a large bowl; stir well. Place in an airtight container and chill 2 hours. **Yield:** 5 servings (serving size: ½ cup).

Summer Chicken Salad with Garden Herbs

Four cups of rotisserie or leftover chicken will work as a time-saver.

1   (3½-pound) whole chicken
¼   cup chopped fresh chives
3   tablespoons white wine vinegar
2   tablespoons capers
2   teaspoons chopped fresh thyme
1   teaspoon chopped fresh oregano
4   teaspoons extravirgin olive oil
½   teaspoon salt
½   teaspoon freshly ground black pepper
1   garlic clove, minced

Carb 0.5g

Calories 172
(29% from fat)
Fat 5.6g
(sat 1.1g)
Protein 28.4g
Fiber 0.3g
Chol 83mg
Iron 1.2mg
Sodium 392mg
Calcium 23mg

1. Remove and discard giblets and neck from chicken. Rinse with cold water. Place chicken in a stockpot; cover with water, and bring to a boil. Reduce heat, and simmer 50 minutes or until tender. Drain, reserving broth for another use. Cool chicken completely. Remove skin from chicken; discard skin. Remove chicken from bones; discard bones and fat. Chop chicken into bite-sized pieces.

2. Combine chives and remaining ingredients in a large bowl. Add chicken; toss well to coat. **Yield:** 6 servings (serving size: ⅔ cup).

> ✳**Lunchtime Safety:** Chicken salad makes a great low-carb, brown-bag lunch, but *only if* it's kept cold until lunchtime. Be sure to keep your salad in a refrigerator or pack it in an insulated cooler with plenty of ice.

Blackened Catfish

Carb 2.9g

Calories 232

(39% from fat)

Fat 10.1g

(sat 2.1g)

Protein 31.6g

Fiber 1g

Chol 99mg

Iron 3.1mg

Sodium 402mg

Calcium 93mg

Double or triple the spice mixture in this recipe, and save the extra to use with other seafood (such as shrimp), chicken, or pork.

2	tablespoons paprika
1	tablespoon dried oregano
½	teaspoon salt
½	teaspoon freshly ground black pepper
¼	teaspoon ground red pepper
4	(6-ounce) farm-raised catfish fillets
2	teaspoons olive oil

1. Combine first 5 ingredients in a small bowl. Sprinkle both sides of fillets with paprika mixture.

2. Heat oil in a large cast-iron skillet over high heat. Add fillets; cook 4 minutes on each side or until fish flakes easily with a fork. **Yield:** 4 servings.

Baked Flounder with Fresh Lemon Pepper
(pictured on cover)

Carb 1.2g

Calories 189

(26% from fat)

Fat 5.4g

(sat 0.9g)

Protein 32.2g

Fiber 0.4g

Chol 82mg

Iron 0.8mg

Sodium 432mg

Calcium 39mg

Use fresh lemon, good olive oil, freshly ground peppercorns, and garlic, and you'll never look at lemon pepper the same way again. Serve with steamed asparagus for a very low-carb dinner.

2	tablespoons grated lemon rind (about 3 lemons)
1	tablespoon extravirgin olive oil
1¼	teaspoons black peppercorns, crushed
½	teaspoon salt
2	garlic cloves, minced
4	(6-ounce) flounder fillets

Cooking spray

Lemon wedges (optional)

1. Preheat oven to 425°.

2. Combine first 5 ingredients. Place fillets on a jelly roll pan coated with cooking spray. Rub garlic mixture evenly over fillets. Bake at 425° for 8 minutes or until fish flakes easily when tested with a fork. Serve with lemon wedges, if desired. **Yield:** 4 servings.

Herb-Crusted Grouper

Substitute dried herbs for fresh, if desired; 1 tablespoon dried equals 3 tablespoons fresh.

4	(6-ounce) grouper fillets
¼	teaspoon seasoned salt (or regular salt)
¼	teaspoon black pepper
	Butter-flavored cooking spray
3	tablespoons chopped fresh basil
3	tablespoons chopped fresh thyme
2	tablespoons chopped fresh parsley
2	teaspoons butter
	Lemon or lime wedges (optional)

Carb 0.8g
Calories 178
(20% from fat)
Fat 3.7g
(sat 1.6g)
Protein 33.2g
Fiber 0.2g
Chol 68mg
Iron 1.7mg
Sodium 206mg
Calcium 73mg

1. Sprinkle fillets on both sides with salt and pepper; coat with cooking spray. Spread herbs on a sheet of wax paper; roll fillets in herbs to coat.

2. Melt butter in a large nonstick skillet over medium heat. Place fillets in skillet; cook 5 minutes on each side or until fish flakes easily when tested with a fork. Serve with lemon or lime wedges, if desired. **Yield:** 4 servings.

Grilled Halibut with Olive Salsa

Carb 2.5g

Calories 221
(28% from fat)
Fat 6.8g
(sat 0.9g)
Protein 35.9g
Fiber 1g
Chol 54mg
Iron 2.4mg
Sodium 585mg
Calcium 105mg

We preferred the briny flavor of the kalamata olives in this salsa, but you can substitute a 2.25-ounce can of chopped ripe olives.

4   (6-ounce) skinless halibut fillets
½   teaspoon salt
¼   teaspoon black pepper
Olive oil-flavored cooking spray
½   cup chopped pitted kalamata olives or chopped ripe olives
2   tablespoons chopped drained oil-packed sun-dried tomato halves
2   tablespoons chopped fresh parsley
½   teaspoon bottled minced garlic

1. Heat a nonstick grill pan over medium-high heat until hot and a drop of water sizzles when dropped on the pan.

2. Sprinkle fillets evenly with salt and pepper; coat with cooking spray. Grill 4 to 5 minutes on each side or until fish flakes easily when tested with a fork.

3. While fish cooks, combine olives and remaining ingredients in a small bowl. Serve salsa over fillets. **Yield:** 4 servings (serving size: 1 fillet and 3 tablespoons salsa).

✳**Watch for the Sizzle:** It's very important to let the grill pan get hot before cooking the fish. The quickest and safest way to check the temperature is with a drop of water. If the water sizzles, the pan is the correct temperature. You'll get the desired golden to dark brown grill marks without overcooking the fish.

Wine-Baked Orange Roughy

To determine if fish is done, prick the thickest part with a fork. The fish will fall apart in flakes and the juices will be milky white if the fish is done.

Carb 2.9g

Calories 128
(9% from fat)
Fat 1.3g
(sat 0g)
Protein 25.4g
Fiber 0.5g
Chol 34mg
Iron 0.7mg
Sodium 258mg
Calcium 59mg

4 (6-ounce) orange roughy fillets (or flounder or sole)
Cooking spray
¼ cup lemon juice
¼ cup dry white wine
¼ teaspoon salt
¼ teaspoon black pepper
⅛ teaspoon garlic powder
¼ cup sliced green onions (about 2 large)
1 (2-ounce) jar diced pimiento, drained

1. Preheat oven to 400°.

2. Place fillets in an 11 x 7-inch baking dish coated with cooking spray; pour lemon juice and wine over fish. Sprinkle fillets evenly with salt, pepper, garlic powder, green onions, and pimiento.

3. Cover and bake at 400° for 10 minutes or until fish flakes easily when tested with a fork. Serve with a slotted spatula. **Yield:** 4 servings.

Sesame Salmon

Carb 0.6g

Calories 292
(47% from fat)
Fat 14.7g
(sat 3.3g)
Protein 36.6g
Fiber 0g
Chol 87mg
Iron 2.3mg
Sodium 213mg
Calcium 21mg

Salmon is naturally high in fat and has a strong, rich flavor. So it needs only a few simple seasonings such as soy sauce and sesame oil and seeds to dress it up. Sesame oil is strong-flavored, so just a small amount makes a flavor impact.

1   tablespoon reduced-sodium soy sauce
1   teaspoon sesame oil
4   (6-ounce) salmon fillets
1½ teaspoons sesame seeds
Cooking spray

1. Combine soy sauce and sesame oil. Brush mixture evenly over salmon fillets. Sprinkle sesame seeds over 1 side of fillets.

2. Heat a large nonstick skillet coated with cooking spray over medium-high heat. Add salmon; cook 4 minutes or until fish flakes easily when tested with a fork, turning once. **Yield:** 4 servings.

Grilled Pesto Salmon

Carb 1g

Calories 280
38% from fat
Fat 11.7g
(sat 2.5g)
Protein 38.9g
Fiber 0.4g
Chol 100mg
Iron 1.9mg
Sodium 360mg
Calcium 108mg

Cooking spray
4   (6-ounce) salmon fillets
¼   teaspoon salt
¼   teaspoon freshly ground black pepper
3   tablespoons commercial pesto
3   tablespoons dry white wine

1. Heat a large grill pan coated with cooking spray over medium heat.

2. Sprinkle fillets evenly with salt and pepper. Set aside.

3. Combine pesto and wine, stirring well.

4. Place fillets on grill pan, and grill 6 minutes on each side or until fish flakes easily when tested with a fork. Serve fish with pesto sauce. **Yield:** 4 servings (serving size: 1 salmon fillet and 1½ tablespoons sauce).

Greek Tuna Steaks

The combination of Mediterranean flavors works equally well not only with the tuna steaks in this recipe, but also with striped bass or red snapper fillets.

Carb 0.2g

Calories 250
(35% from fat)
Fat 9.7g
(sat 2.3g)
Protein 38.2g
Fiber 0.1g
Chol 63mg
Iron 1.8mg
Sodium 357mg
Calcium 4mg

1½   teaspoons chopped fresh or ½ teaspoon dried oregano
 1   teaspoon olive oil
¾   teaspoon chopped fresh or ¼ teaspoon dried thyme
½   teaspoon salt
¼   teaspoon black pepper
 4   (6-ounce) tuna steaks (about ¾ inch thick)
Cooking spray
 4   lemon wedges

1. Combine first 5 ingredients in a small bowl; rub herb mixture evenly over tuna steaks. Cover tuna steaks, and chill 15 minutes.

2. Heat a large grill pan coated with cooking spray over medium-high heat. Add tuna steaks; cook 5 minutes on each side or until desired degree of doneness. Serve tuna steaks with lemon wedges. **Yield:** 4 servings.

Southern-Style Shrimp
(pictured on back cover)

Carb 3.6g

Calories 218
(22% from fat)
Fat 5.2g
(sat 2.4g)
Protein 37.9g
Fiber 1g
Chol 341mg
Iron 6.2mg
Sodium 586mg
Calcium 81mg

1 tablespoon butter
2 tablespoons packaged real bacon pieces
  (such as Hormel), divided
1 teaspoon bottled minced garlic
1½ pounds peeled and deveined large shrimp
1 (8-ounce) package sliced mushrooms
¼ cup sliced green onions
¼ teaspoon salt
½ teaspoon hot pepper sauce
¼ cup chopped fresh parsley
1 tablespoon lemon juice

1. Melt butter in a large nonstick skillet over medium-high heat. Add 1 tablespoon bacon pieces and garlic; sauté 1 minute. Add shrimp; sauté 3 minutes. Add mushrooms; cook 2 to 3 minutes or until mushrooms are tender and shrimp is done, stirring frequently. Stir in onions, salt, and hot sauce; remove from heat. Stir in parsley and lemon juice. Sprinkle with 1 tablespoon bacon pieces. **Yield:** 4 servings (serving size: about 1 cup).

✳**Quick Shrimp:** Did you know that most grocery stores sell raw shrimp that has been peeled and deveined? You may have to ask, but it will be well worth the time you save. When shopping remember that 1 pound of unpeeled shrimp yields about ¾ pound of peeled and deveined shrimp.

Southwestern Grilled Flank Steak

A homemade spice mix takes just a minute or two to assemble and gives flank steak a real flavor boost.

1 (1½-pound) lean flank steak (about ¾ inch thick)
2 tablespoons Hungarian sweet paprika
1 tablespoon chili powder
2 teaspoons ground cumin
1 teaspoon ground cinnamon
½ teaspoon salt
Cooking spray

Carb 2.6g
Calories 271
(55% from fat)
Fat 16.5g
(sat 6.9g)
Protein 27.5g
Fiber 1.1g
Chol 74mg
Iron 4mg
Sodium 298mg
Calcium 25mg

1. Trim excess fat from steak. Combine paprika and next 4 ingredients; rub over both sides of steak. Place steak in a dish; cover and chill at least 4 hours.

2. Prepare grill.

3. Remove steak from dish. Place steak on grill rack coated with cooking spray; cover and grill 4 minutes on each side or until desired degree of doneness. Remove steak from grill; let stand 5 minutes before slicing. Cut steak diagonally across the grain into thin slices. **Yield:** 6 servings (serving size: 3 ounces).

Port Marinated Steaks

Carb 3.6g

Calories 191
(32% from fat)
Fat 6.7g
(sat 2.6g)
Protein 27.9g
Fiber 1.2g
Chol 80mg
Iron 4.6mg
Sodium 111mg
Calcium 53mg

Steak marinated in port, a sweet red wine with a bit of brandy added to it, takes on an especially unique flavor. Port has a higher carbohydrate content than dry red wine, but because of its strong flavor, only a small amount is needed. Here, each serving gets about 2½ grams carbohydrate from the port.

1½   pounds lean boneless top sirloin steak
½   cup port or sweet red wine
2   tablespoons Worcestershire sauce
2   tablespoons balsamic vinegar
2   garlic cloves, crushed
3   tablespoons minced fresh thyme
Cooking spray

1. Trim fat from steak. Combine wine and next 4 ingredients in a heavy-duty, zip-top plastic bag. Add steak; seal bag, and turn bag to coat steak. Marinate in refrigerator 8 hours, turning bag occasionally.

2. Remove steak from marinade; pour marinade into a small saucepan. Bring marinade to a boil; boil until reduced to ¼ cup. Set aside.

3. Prepare grill.

4. Place steak on grill rack coated with cooking spray; cover and grill 5 minutes on each side or to desired degree of doneness. Let steak stand 5 minutes. Cut diagonally across grain into thin slices; drizzle with hot marinade. **Yield:** 6 servings.

Spiced Pepper-Crusted Filet Mignon with Asparagus
(pictured on back cover)

Guests will leave your dinner table satisfied. They'll never guess you're "counting carbs."

1 teaspoon bottled minced garlic
½ teaspoon olive oil
½ teaspoon salt, divided
12 ounces fresh asparagus, trimmed
1 tablespoon cracked black pepper
2 teaspoons brandy
½ teaspoon garlic powder
4 (4-ounce) beef tenderloin steaks (about 1 inch thick)
Cooking spray

Carb 4.7g

Calories 269
(39% from fat)
Fat 11.6g
(sat 4.1g)
Protein 34.9g
Fiber 1.2g
Chol 95mg
Iron 5.1mg
Sodium 367mg
Calcium 36mg

1. Preheat broiler.

2. Combine minced garlic, olive oil, ¼ teaspoon salt, and asparagus in a large bowl, tossing gently to coat.

3. Combine ¼ teaspoon salt, pepper, brandy, and garlic powder; rub evenly over steaks. Place steaks on a broiler pan coated with cooking spray; broil 6 minutes. Turn steaks over; add asparagus to pan. Broil 5 minutes or until desired degree of doneness. **Yield:** 4 servings (serving size: 1 steak and 3 ounces asparagus).

Peppery Mushroom Burgers

For a family meal, serve whole wheat hamburger buns. Each bun weighs in at about 15 grams of carbohydrate.

1   (8-ounce) package sliced mushrooms, divided
1   pound lean ground round
2   teaspoons instant minced onion
2   teaspoons low-sodium Worcestershire sauce
1   teaspoon freshly ground black pepper
Cooking spray
¼   cup dry red wine or low-salt beef broth
¼   cup water

1. Coarsely chop 1½ cups sliced mushrooms. Combine beef, chopped mushrooms, onion, and Worcestershire sauce in a bowl; shape into 4 equal patties, ¼ inch thick. Sprinkle pepper evenly on both sides of patties.

2. Heat a 12-inch nonstick skillet coated with cooking spray over medium-high heat. Add patties, and cook 5 to 6 minutes on each side or until done. Transfer to a serving platter, and keep warm.

3. Add wine, water, and remaining mushrooms to skillet; cook, stirring constantly, over medium heat about 3 minutes or until mushrooms are tender, scraping particles that cling to bottom. Pour mushroom mixture over patties. **Yield:** 4 servings.

Rosemary-Grilled Veal Chops
(pictured on back cover)

4 (6-ounce) lean veal loin chops (¾ inch thick)
Olive oil-flavored cooking spray
1½ teaspoons dried rosemary, crushed
¾ teaspoon lemon pepper

1. Prepare grill.

2. Trim fat from veal. Coat both sides of veal with cooking spray. Combine rosemary and lemon-pepper seasoning; rub evenly over veal.

3. Place veal on grill rack coated with cooking spray; cover and grill 5 to 6 minutes on each side or until done. **Yield:** 4 servings.

Carb 0.3g
Calories 187
(51% from fat)
Fat 10.7g
(saturated 4.5g)
Protein 21.1g
Fiber 0.1g
Chol 88mg
Iron 0.9mg
Sodium 140mg
Calcium 21mg

Mustard-Garlic Lamb Chops

2 garlic cloves, minced
½ teaspoon black pepper
¼ teaspoon dried thyme
⅛ teaspoon salt
2 teaspoons fresh lemon juice
2 teaspoons Dijon mustard
1 teaspoon olive oil
4 (5-ounce) lean lamb loin chops
Cooking spray

1. Prepare broiler.

2. Combine first 4 ingredients in a small bowl; mash with back of a spoon until mixture forms a paste. Stir in lemon juice, mustard, and olive oil.

3. Trim fat from chops. Spread garlic mixture over both sides of chops. Place chops on a broiler pan coated with cooking spray. Broil 6 to 7 minutes on each side or to desired degree of doneness. **Yield:** 4 servings.

Carb 1.1g
Calories 192
(44% from fat)
Fat 9.3g
(sat 3g)
Protein 24.3g
Fiber 0.1g
Chol 77mg
Iron 1.8mg
Sodium 216mg
Calcium 21mg

Balsamic Pork Chops

Carb 4.7g

Calories 220
(47% from fat)
Fat 11.5g
(sat 4.3g)
Protein 22.9g
Fiber 0g
Chol 69mg
Iron 1.1mg
Sodium 107mg
Calcium 30mg

A staple in the Italian pantry, balsamic vinegar guarantees that these pork chops will be some of the most flavorful you'll ever eat.

4   (4-ounce) boneless center-cut pork loin chops
      (½ inch thick)
1   teaspoon salt-free lemon-herb seasoning
Cooking spray
½   cup balsamic vinegar
⅓   cup fat-free, less-sodium chicken broth

1. Trim fat from chops. Sprinkle chops evenly on both sides with seasoning. Heat a medium nonstick skillet coated with cooking spray over medium-high heat. Add chops, and cook 3 to 4 minutes on each side or until lightly browned. Remove chops from skillet, and keep warm.

2. Wipe drippings from skillet with a paper towel. Combine vinegar and broth in skillet. Cook over medium-high heat until mixture is reduced to a thin sauce (about 5 to 6 minutes), stirring occasionally. Spoon sauce over chops. **Yield:** 4 servings.

Pork Medallions with Mustard Sauce

Change the flavor of this recipe by substituting different flavors of mustard such as brown, sweet-hot, or honey mustard.

1   pound pork tenderloin
1   teaspoon vegetable oil
Cooking spray
½   cup fat-free milk
2   tablespoons Dijon mustard
3   green onions, sliced

Carb 2.4g
Calories 160
(26% from fat)
Fat 4.7g
(sat 1.2g)
Protein 24.9g
Fiber 0.2g
Chol 74mg
Iron 1.6mg
Sodium 295mg
Calcium 50mg

1. Trim fat from pork. Cut pork into 1-inch-thick slices. Place slices between two sheets of heavy-duty plastic wrap; flatten to ½-inch thickness, using a meat mallet or rolling pin.

2. Heat oil in a large nonstick skillet coated with cooking spray over medium-high heat. Add half of pork medallions, and cook 3 minutes on each side or until browned. Remove pork from skillet; set aside, and keep warm. Repeat procedure with remaining half of pork medallions.

3. Reduce heat to low; add milk to skillet, stirring constantly, scraping particles that cling to bottom. Stir in mustard and green onions. Return pork to skillet; cover and cook 2 minutes, turning to coat with sauce. **Yield:** 4 servings.

Lemon-Herb Roasted Chicken

Carb 1.8g

Calories 105
(23% from fat)
Fat 2.7g
(sat 0.7g)
Protein 17.6g
Fiber 0.5g
Chol 57mg
Iron 1.1mg
Sodium 161mg
Calcium 27mg

1 (3-pound) roasting chicken
3 sprigs fresh rosemary, thyme, or sage
2 tablespoons chopped fresh rosemary, thyme, or sage
1 teaspoon grated lemon rind
3 tablespoons fresh lemon juice
¼ teaspoon salt
¼ teaspoon black pepper
2 garlic cloves, minced

1. Preheat oven to 400°.

2. Remove and discard giblets from chicken. Rinse chicken under cold water; pat dry. Trim excess fat. Starting at neck cavity, loosen skin from breast and drumsticks by inserting fingers, gently pushing between skin and meat.

3. Place fresh rosemary, thyme, or sage sprigs under loosened skin over breast. Combine chopped rosemary and remaining 5 ingredients; brush over chicken and in cavity of chicken.

4. Place chicken on a rack in roasting pan. Insert meat thermometer into meaty part of thigh, making sure not to touch bone.

5. Bake, uncovered, at 400° for 1 hour or until thermometer registers 180°. Let stand 15 minutes before serving. **Yield:** 6 servings.

✳**Safe Poultry:** To prevent food-borne illnesses, poultry must be cooked to 180°. For whole birds, use an instant-read thermometer inserted in the thickest part of the thigh to confirm the temperature. Another test is to pierce poultry parts with the tip of a knife—the flesh should be opaque and the juices clear when done.

Spiced Chicken Thighs

Garam masala, a blend of spices used in Indian cooking, adds a touch of warmth to this flavorful dish. Purchase garam masala in Indian food markets or in the gourmet or spice section of some supermarkets,

Carb 3.9g
Calories 203
(30% from fat)
Fat 6.7g
(sat 1.6g)
Protein 29.9g
Fiber 1.1g
Chol 121mg
Iron 2.1mg
Sodium 536mg
Calcium 35mg

¾   teaspoon olive oil
Cooking spray
1   cup vertically sliced onion
2   teaspoons garam masala
½   teaspoon salt
¼   teaspoon curry powder
8   chicken thighs (about 2¼ pounds), skinned
¼   cup dry red wine
2   tablespoons red wine vinegar
1   cup fat-free, less-sodium chicken broth
3   tablespoons chopped fresh parsley

1. Heat oil in a 12-inch nonstick skillet coated with cooking spray over medium-high heat. Add onion; sauté 3 minutes. Remove from pan.

2. Combine garam masala, salt, and curry powder; sprinkle evenly over chicken. Add chicken to pan; cook over medium-high heat 4 minutes on each side or until browned. Add wine and vinegar; cook 30 seconds, scraping pan to loosen browned bits. Add onion and broth; bring to a boil. Cover, reduce heat, and simmer 20 minutes or until chicken is done; stir in parsley. **Yield:** 4 servings (serving size: 2 thighs and about ⅓ cup sauce).

Chicken with Two-Olive Topping

Carb 3.2g

Calories 159
(22% from fat)
Fat 3.9g
(sat 0.8g)
Protein 26.7g
Fiber 1g
Chol 66mg
Iron 1.7mg
Sodium 390mg
Calcium 30mg

We've used two varieties of olives to make a chunky, salsa-textured topping. Any combination of good olives will work well.

1   red bell pepper
1   orange bell pepper
1   yellow bell pepper
6   (4-ounce) skinless, boneless chicken breast halves
¾   teaspoon kosher salt
¼   teaspoon freshly ground black pepper
2   teaspoons olive oil, divided
2   teaspoons chopped fresh rosemary
2   garlic cloves, minced
3   tablespoons chopped pitted kalamata olives
3   tablespoons chopped pitted green olives
2   teaspoons fresh lemon juice

1. Preheat broiler.

2. Cut bell peppers in half lengthwise; discard seeds and membranes. Place pepper halves, skin sides up, on a foil-lined baking sheet; flatten with hand. Broil 10 minutes or until blackened. Place in a zip-top plastic bag; seal. Let stand 10 minutes. Peel and chop.

3. Sprinkle chicken with salt and black pepper. Heat 1 teaspoon oil in a large nonstick skillet over medium-high heat. Add chicken; cook 5 minutes on each side or until done. Remove from pan; keep warm.

4. Add 1 teaspoon oil, rosemary, and garlic to pan; sauté 30 seconds or until garlic begins to brown. Stir in bell peppers, olives, and lemon juice; cook 1 minute or until thoroughly heated, stirring constantly. **Yield:** 6 servings (serving size: 1 chicken breast half and ⅓ cup sauce).

Lemon-Pepper Chicken

4 (4-ounce) skinless, boneless chicken breast
    halves
1¼ teaspoons lemon-pepper
1 teaspoon olive oil
Cooking spray
¼ cup fat-free, less-sodium chicken broth
¼ cup balsamic vinegar

Carb 0.3g
Calories 138
(18% from fat)
Fat 2.7g
(sat 0.5g)
Protein 26.2g
Fiber 0g
Chol 66mg
Iron 0.9mg
Sodium 233mg
Calcium 13mg

1. Sprinkle chicken breasts evenly with lemon-pepper. Heat oil in a large nonstick skillet coated with cooking spray over medium-high heat. Add chicken to skillet, and cook 4 to 5 minutes on each side or until chicken is done. Transfer chicken to a serving platter; keep warm.

2. Add broth and vinegar to skillet; cook, stirring constantly, 1 minute or until slightly thickened. Spoon sauce over chicken. **Yield:** 4 servings.

Grilled Caribbean Chicken

4 (4-ounce) skinless, boneless chicken breast
    halves
2 teaspoons lime juice
1 teaspoon vegetable oil
2 teaspoons jerk seasoning
Cooking spray

Carb 1.4g
Calories 153
(25% from fat)
Fat 4.2g
(sat 1g)
Protein 25.9g
Fiber 0.2g
Chol 70mg
Iron 0.8mg
Sodium 97mg
Calcium 13 mg

1. Prepare grill.

2. Place chicken between 2 sheets of heavy-duty plastic wrap, and flatten to ¼-inch thickness, using a meat mallet or rolling pin. Combine lime juice and oil; brush over both sides of chicken. Rub both sides of chicken with jerk seasoning.

3. Place chicken on grill rack coated with cooking spray; grill, covered, 5 to 6 minutes on each side or until done. **Yield:** 4 servings.

Turkey Cutlets with Rosemary-Tomato Sauce

Carb 3.6g

Calories 182
(27% from fat)
Fat 5.5g
(sat 0.9g)
Protein 28.6g
Fiber 0.9g
Chol 70mg
Iron 1.8mg
Sodium 498mg
Calcium 19mg

Fresh tomatoes really make a difference in this simple, chunky sauce.

4	teaspoons olive oil, divided
8	(2-ounce) turkey cutlets
¾	teaspoon salt, divided
½	teaspoon black pepper, divided
1	tablespoon chopped fresh rosemary
1	teaspoon bottled minced garlic
1½	cups chopped tomato
1	tablespoon white wine vinegar

1. Heat 2 teaspoons oil in a large nonstick skillet over medium-high heat. Sprinkle turkey with ¼ teaspoon salt and ¼ teaspoon pepper. Add turkey to pan; cook 2 minutes on each side or until done. Remove from pan; keep warm.

2. Add 2 teaspoons oil, rosemary, and garlic to pan; sauté 1 minute. Add tomato; cook 1 minute, stirring frequently. Stir in ½ teaspoon salt, ¼ teaspoon pepper, and vinegar. Serve over turkey. **Yield:** 4 servings (serving size: 2 turkey cutlets and ¼ cup sauce).

Roasted Asparagus with Balsamic Browned Butter

40 asparagus spears, trimmed (about 2 pounds)
Cooking spray
¼ teaspoon kosher salt
⅛ teaspoon black pepper
2 tablespoons butter
2 teaspoons low-sodium soy sauce
1 teaspoon balsamic vinegar

1. Preheat oven to 400°.

2. Arrange asparagus in a single layer on baking sheet; coat with cooking spray. Sprinkle with salt and pepper. Bake at 400° for 12 minutes or until tender.

3. Melt butter in a small skillet over medium heat; cook 3 minutes or until lightly browned, shaking pan occasionally. Remove from heat; stir in soy sauce and vinegar. Drizzle over asparagus, tossing well to coat. Serve immediately. **Yield:** 8 servings (serving size: 5 spears).

Carb 3.9g
Calories 45
(60% from fat)
Fat 3g
(sat 1.8g)
Protein 1.9g
Fiber 1.7g
Chol 8mg
Iron 0.7mg
Sodium 134mg
Calcium 18mg

✳**A Pantry Essential:** Be sure to keep a bottle of balsamic vinegar in your pantry. Its versatility is endless, and its full-bodied flavor tastes slightly sweet with a hint of tartness. Use balsamic vinegar to jazz up sautéed vegetables, splash on salad greens, and sprinkle over grilled chicken.

Green Beans with Crushed Walnuts

Carb 5.8g

Calories 52
(52% from fat)
Fat 3g
(sat 1g)
Protein 1.8g
Fiber 2.8g
Chol 3mg
Iron 0.9mg
Sodium 213mg
Calcium 31mg

This simple dish relies on freshly ground nutmeg. Look for whole nutmeg in the spice aisle, and store it in the freezer for up to a year.

1¼ pounds green beans, trimmed
2 teaspoons butter
2 tablespoons finely crushed walnuts
½ teaspoon salt
¼ teaspoon freshly ground whole nutmeg

1. Place beans in a large saucepan of boiling water; cook 5 minutes. Drain.

2. Heat butter in a large nonstick skillet over medium-high heat. Add walnuts; sauté 1 minute, stirring constantly. Add beans, salt, and nutmeg; cook 1 minute. **Yield:** 6 servings (serving size: ⅔ cup).

Sesame Steamed Broccoli

Carb 5g

Calories 54
(36% from fat)
Fat 2g
(sat 0.3g)
Protein 3.1g
Fiber 2.6g
Chol 0mg
Iron 2.9g
Sodium 398mg
Calcium 41mg

1 (12-ounce) package broccoli florets (about 4½ cups)
1½ teaspoons dark sesame oil
2 tablespoons low-sodium soy sauce
⅛ teaspoon salt
¼ teaspoon freshly ground black pepper
2 teaspoons sesame seeds, toasted

1. Steam broccoli, covered, 6 minutes or until crisp-tender.

2. Combine oil and remaining 4 ingredients. Pour oil mixture over broccoli; toss. **Yield:** 4 servings (serving size: 1 cup).

Pesto-Tossed Cauliflower

Turn steamed cauliflower into a special side dish by tossing the florets in pesto.

4	cups cauliflower florets
½	cup water
2½	tablespoons commercial pesto
¼	teaspoon salt
¼	teaspoon freshly ground black pepper

1. Place cauliflower in a microwave-safe bowl; pour water over cauliflower. Cover with plastic wrap; vent. Microwave at HIGH 6 minutes or until done.

2. Drain cauliflower, and return to dish. Add pesto, salt, and pepper; toss well. Cover; microwave at HIGH 1 minute or until hot. **Yield:** 4 servings (serving size: 1 cup).

Carb 5.9g

Calories 74
(57% from fat)
Fat 4.7g
(sat 1.2g)
Protein 3.8g
Fiber 2.8g
Chol 3mg
Iron 0.8mg
Sodium 252mg
Calcium 92mg

✳**Plenty of Pesto:** Pesto has a very concentrated flavor, so a small amount goes a long way. That makes it ideal for shortcut cooking. (One tablespoon pesto has about 1½ to 2 grams carbohydrate.) To store leftover pesto, spoon it into ice cube trays and freeze; store frozen cubes in a zip-top plastic freezer bag for up to a month. One cube of frozen pesto is equivalent to about 2 tablespoons of fresh.

Cumin-Scented Squash

Carb 3.9g

Calories 48
(68% from fat)
Fat 3.6g
(sat 0.5g)
Protein 1.1g
Fiber 1.7g
Chol 0mg
Iron 0.5mg
Sodium 149mg
Calcium 19mg

Pungent, sharp, and slightly bitter, cumin is a common ingredient in Indian spice blends and Mexican foods. Like other spices, it should be stored in a cool place, away from heat.

2   fresh yellow squash, halved lengthwise
1   tablespoon olive oil
¼   teaspoon ground cumin
¼   teaspoon salt
⅛   teaspoon ground red pepper

1. Preheat oven to 450°.

2. Place squash halves, cut side up, on a baking sheet; drizzle with oil. Bake at 450° for 20 minutes.

3. Cook cumin in a small skillet over medium heat, stirring and shaking often, 3 to 4 minutes or until fragrant. Combine cumin, salt, and red pepper in a small bowl. Sprinkle over squash. **Yield:** 4 servings (serving size: 1 squash half).

Skillet Zucchini

Carb 2.3g

Calories 16
(28% from fat)
Fat 0.5g
(sat 0.3g)
Protein 1.3g
Fiber 0.3g
Chol 1mg
Iron 0.5mg
Sodium 318mg
Calcium 38mg

Olive oil-flavored cooking spray
1   teaspoon bottled minced garlic
2   large zucchini, sliced and halved
½   teaspoon salt
¼   teaspoon black pepper
1   tablespoon grated Parmesan cheese

1. Heat a large nonstick skillet coated with cooking spray over medium heat. Add garlic, and sauté 1 minute. Add zucchini; sprinkle with salt and pepper. Cook until zucchini is tender, stirring occasionally. Sprinkle with Parmesan cheese. **Yield:** 4 servings (serving size: ½ cup).

Cucumbers Vinaigrette

3   cucumbers, peeled, halved lengthwise, seeded, and thinly sliced (about 3½ cups)
½   cup vertically sliced red onion
1   tablespoon chopped fresh or 1 teaspoon dried basil
1   tablespoon chopped fresh or 1 teaspoon dried parsley
2   tablespoons red wine vinegar
1   tablespoon olive oil
2½   teaspoons Dijon mustard
¼   teaspoon salt

Carb 2.9g
Calories 35
(67% from fat)
Fat 2.6g
(sat 0.4g)
Protein 0.7g
Fiber 0.7g
Chol 0mg
Iron 0.3mg
Sodium 153mg
Calcium 16mg

1. Place cucumbers and onion in a bowl. Combine basil and remaining ingredients; pour over cucumber mixture. Toss gently. Cover and chill. **Yield:** 6 servings (serving size: ½ cup).

✳**Fresh Herbs:** There's really no comparison between dried and fresh herbs. Once you start using fresh, you won't go back. When shopping for fresh, look for herbs with vibrant colors and fragrant aromas.

Don't wash herbs until you're ready to use them. Instead, wrap the stems in a damp paper towel and store loosely in a zip-top plastic bag. (Or seal the towel-wrapped herbs in a roomy plastic container.) Keep delicate herbs like dill and cilantro refrigerated, and use as soon as possible. Hardier herbs like rosemary and sage will stay fresh for a week or two. Since fresh basil often turns black when refrigerated, store it at room temperature in a jar with an inch or so of water. It will stay bright and green for several days.

Marinated Tomatoes

Carb 4.7g

Calories 62
(68% from fat)
Fat 4.7g
(sat 1.3g)
Protein 1.5g
Fiber 0.8g
Chol 6mg
Iron 0.6mg
Sodium 205mg
Calcium 41mg

Fabulous when made with ripe red tomatoes, this side salad will quickly become a summer favorite.

4	ripe tomatoes, sliced
¼	cup fat-free vinaigrette
¼	cup (1 ounce) crumbled feta cheese

Freshly ground black pepper (optional)

1. Combine tomato and vinaigrette. Cover and chill at least 1 hour. Sprinkle with feta cheese and freshly ground pepper, if desired. **Yield:** 4 servings.

Mediterranean Tossed Salad

Carb 4.9g

Calories 67
(55% from fat)
Fat 4.1g
(sat 2.1g)
Protein 3.3g
Fiber 1.3g
Chol 10mg
Iron 1.1mg
Sodium 222mg
Calcium 45mg

If the basil-and-tomato-feta cheese isn't available, substitute peppercorn feta or plain feta.

6	cups torn green leaf lettuce
½	cup thinly sliced red onion (about 1 small)
¼	cup sliced ripe olives
½	cup (2 ounces) crumbled feta cheese with basil and tomato
1	teaspoon dried oregano
⅓	cup fat-free vinaigrette

1. Combine lettuce, onion, olives, cheese, and oregano in a large bowl; pour vinaigrette over salad, and toss gently. Serve immediately. **Yield:** 4 servings.

Mixed Greens with Bacon-Horseradish Dressing

6 slices turkey bacon
½ cup low-fat buttermilk
2 tablespoons fat-free mayonnaise
1 teaspoon prepared horseradish
⅛ teaspoon salt
⅛ teaspoon freshly ground black pepper
6 cups torn mixed salad greens
1 cup sliced fresh mushrooms
Freshly ground black pepper (optional)

Carb 3.4g
Calories 126
(52% from fat)
Fat 7.3g
(sat 1.9g)
Protein 8.7g
Fiber 0.9g
Chol 36mg
Iron 0.6mg
Sodium 844mg
Calcium 42mg

1. Place bacon on a microwave-safe plate lined with paper towels. Microwave at HIGH 5 minutes. Crumble bacon.

2. Combine buttermilk and next 4 ingredients, stirring well.

3. Combine salad greens and mushrooms; arrange evenly on 6 salad plates. Spoon 2 tablespoons buttermilk dressing over each salad; sprinkle evenly with bacon. Sprinkle with additional freshly ground pepper, if desired. **Yield:** 6 servings.

✳**Clean Greens:** Store leafy greens unwashed in plastic bags in the refrigerator. When you're ready to use them, you'll need to wash the greens thoroughly since they harbor sand and other debris. Avoid using a colander because just running water over the leaves isn't enough to clean them.

Instead, dunk greens in a large bowl or sink filled with cold water. The dirt will sink to the bottom while the greens float to the top. Remove the leaves by hand, and place them in another bowl. Pour out the water and repeat the procedure until the water is free of debris.

Roasted Red Pepper Dip

Carb 2g

Calories 38
(59% from fat)
Fat 2.3g
(sat 1.6g)
Protein 1.6g
Fiber 0.1g
Chol 6.6mg
Iron 0.1mg
Sodium 168mg
Calcium 20mg

2   (5½-ounce) bottles roasted red bell peppers, drained
1   tablespoon balsamic vinegar
¼   teaspoon salt
⅛   teaspoon ground red pepper
1   (8-ounce) tub light cream cheese
1   garlic clove

1. Pat roasted peppers dry with paper towels.

2. Place all ingredients in a food processor; process until smooth, scraping sides of bowl if necessary. Cover and chill 2 hours. **Yield: 16** servings (serving size: 2 tablespoons).

Cream Cheese and Pesto Spread

Carb 1g

Calories 46
(64% from fat)
Fat 3.3g
(sat 1.6g)
Protein 2.9g
Fiber 0.1g
Chol 9mg
Iron 0.2mg
Sodium 116mg
Calcium 47mg

Keep these five ingredients in your pantry or refrigerator and you'll never be at a loss for a quick snack or appetizer.

1   (8-ounce) block ⅓-less-fat cream cheese, softened
2   tablespoons commercial pesto
2   tablespoons grated fresh Parmesan cheese
1   tablespoon chopped ripe olives
1   tablespoon diced pimiento

1. Combine cream cheese, pesto, and Parmesan cheese in a small bowl; beat with a mixer at medium speed until blended. Stir in olives and pimiento. Cover and chill at least 1 hour. Serve with celery sticks. **Yield: 12** servings (serving size: 2 tablespoons).

Garlic Herb Cheese Spread

1½ cups fat-free sour cream
½ cup light cream cheese
1 tablespoon minced fresh chives
2 teaspoons minced fresh parsley
½ teaspoon salt
½ teaspoon black pepper
1 small garlic clove, minced, or ½ teaspoon
   bottled minced garlic

Carb 2.2g
Calories 32
(34% from fat)
Fat 1.2g
(sat 0.8g)
Protein 2.4g
Fiber 0g
Chol 4mg
Iron 0mg
Sodium 130mg
Calcium 36mg

1. Combine sour cream and cream cheese in a bowl; stir well. Stir in chives and remaining ingredients; cover and chill at least 1 hour.

2. Spoon spread into hollowed out cherry tomatoes or mushroom caps. To store, cover cheese spread, and refrigerate up to 4 days. **Yield:** 16 servings (serving size: 2 tablespoons).

✳**Low Carb Dipping:** Keep your carbs at a minimum by enjoying these dips and spreads with low-carbohydrate vegetables: mushrooms, endive, bell peppers, celery, and jícama.

Deviled Eggs

Carb 1.3g

Calories 38
(50% from fat)
Fat 2.1g
(sat 0.6g)
Protein 3.1g
Fiber 0g
Chol 80mg
Iron 0.3mg
Sodium 82mg
Calcium 21mg

Prepare the eggs up to 24 hours in advance, then store, covered, in the refrigerator or cooler until ready to serve.

12 large eggs
⅓ cup plain fat-free yogurt
3 tablespoons low-fat mayonnaise
1 tablespoon Dijon mustard
1 to 2 teaspoons hot pepper sauce
⅛ teaspoon salt
⅛ teaspoon paprika
⅛ teaspoon black pepper
2 tablespoons chopped green onions (optional)

1. Place eggs in a large saucepan. Cover with water to 1 inch above eggs; bring just to a boil. Remove from heat; cover and let stand 15 minutes. Drain and rinse with cold running water until cool. Remove shells; slice eggs in half lengthwise, and remove yolks. Reserve 3 yolks for other uses.

2. Combine yogurt and next 4 ingredients in a medium bowl. Add remaining 9 yolks; beat with a mixer at high speed until smooth. Spoon about 1 tablespoon yolk mixture into each egg white half. Cover and chill 1 hour. Sprinkle with paprika and black pepper. Garnish with green onions, if desired. **Yield:** 24 servings (serving size: 1 egg half).

Mini Frittatas with Ham and Cheese

Bake these bite-sized frittatas in a miniature muffin pan. They taste great hot or at room temperature, so you can make them in advance.

Cooking spray
½   cup finely chopped onion
⅔   cup chopped reduced-fat ham (about 2 ounces)
⅓   cup (about 1½ ounces) shredded reduced-fat extrasharp Cheddar cheese
2   tablespoons chopped fresh chives
⅛   teaspoon dried thyme
⅛   teaspoon black pepper
4   large egg whites
1   large egg

Carb 2.3g
Calories 39
(30% from fat)
Fat 1.3g
(sat 0.5g)
Protein 4.4g
Fiber 0.4g
Chol 32mg
Iron 0.2mg
Sodium 121mg
Calcium 80mg

1. Preheat oven to 350°.

2. Heat a large nonstick skillet coated with cooking spray over medium-high heat. Add onion; sauté 2 minutes or until crisp-tender. Add ham; sauté 3 minutes. Remove from heat; cool 5 minutes.

3. Combine cheese and remaining 5 ingredients in a large bowl; stir with a whisk. Add ham mixture, stirring with a whisk. Spoon mixture into 24 miniature muffin cups coated with cooking spray. Bake at 350° for 20 minutes or until set. **Yield:** 8 servings (serving size: 3 frittatas).

Tuna Salad Bites

Carb 3.3g

Calories 31
(20% from fat)
Fat 0.7g
(sat 0.1g)
Protein 3.3g
Fiber 0.7g
Chol 5mg
Iron 0.3mg
Sodium 79mg
Calcium 11mg

1   (6-ounce) can low-sodium, low-fat chunk white tuna in water, drained
½   cup finely chopped carrot
⅓   cup thinly sliced green onions
¼   cup sliced pimiento-stuffed olives
¼   cup low-fat mayonnaise
3   tablespoons minced fresh parsley
1   tablespoon lemon juice
½   teaspoon black pepper
2   medium cucumbers, cut into ½-inch slices

1. Combine first 8 ingredients in a medium bowl, stirring well. Cover and chill at least 1 hour.

2. Scoop out a hollow space in center of 1 side of each cucumber slice, using a ½-teaspoon circular measuring spoon or a small melon baller. Fill centers of cucumber slices with tuna mixture. Serve immediately. **Yield:** 12 servings (serving size: 1 appetizer).

Party Shrimp

Carb 0.6g

Calories 37
(36% from fat)
Fat 1.4g
(sat 0.2g)
Protein 5.1g
Fiber 0.1g
Chol 47mg
Iron 0.8mg
Sodium 103mg
Calcium 10mg

To save time, purchase fresh steamed and peeled shrimp from your grocery.

⅓   cup finely chopped fresh parsley
3   tablespoons finely chopped green onions
3   tablespoons minced red onion
2   tablespoons lemon juice
1   tablespoon extravirgin olive oil
¼   teaspoon salt
⅛   teaspoon ground red pepper
1   pound large shrimp, cooked and peeled

1. Combine first 7 ingredients; add shrimp, tossing well. Cover and chill at least 3 hours. **Yield:** 12 servings (serving size: approximately 3 shrimp).

Asian Marinated Asparagus

1 pound asparagus spears (about 20 spears)
2 tablespoons water
¼ cup seasoned rice vinegar
2 tablespoons soy sauce
2 teaspoons bottled chopped fresh ginger (such as Christopher Ranch)
1 teaspoon dark sesame oil

Carb 4.9g
Calories 38
(31% from fat)
Fat 1.3g
(sat 0.2g)
Protein 2.5g
Fiber 1.8g
Chol 0mg
Iron 0.9mg
Sodium 518mg
Calcium 20mg

1. Snap off tough ends of asparagus, and remove scales with a knife or vegetable peeler, if desired. Place asparagus spears and water in a shallow microwave-safe dish. Cover and microwave at HIGH 2 to 4 minutes or until asparagus is crisp-tender; drain. Return asparagus to dish.

2. Combine vinegar and next 3 ingredients in a small bowl; stir with a whisk until mixture is blended. Pour vinegar mixture over asparagus, turning asparagus to coat. Cover and marinate in refrigerator at least 2 hours, turning asparagus occasionally. **Yield:** 4 servings (serving size: 5 spears).

> ✳**Low-carb Snacktime:** Keep your carb count under control at snacktime by enjoying cheese (such as Cheddar and mozzarella), cream cheese-stuffed celery, nuts, seeds (such as sunflower seeds), and raw vegetables (such as mushrooms, celery, and cucumber).

Index